DON'T GET SCREWED BY THE IR$

DON'T GET SCREWED BY THE IRS
How to Reduce What You Owe and Stay Out of Tax Trouble for Good

ISBN: 978-1-964046-42-6

Expert Press
www.ExpertPress.net

Editing by Chelsea Morning
Copyediting by Lucy Spencer
Proofreading by Heather Dubnick
Text design and composition by Emily Fritz
Cover design by Casey Fritz

DON'T GET SCREWED BY THE IRS

HOW TO REDUCE WHAT YOU OWE AND STAY OUT OF TAX TROUBLE FOR GOOD

RON FRIEDMAN
THE TAX RELIEF PRO

DISCLAIMER

This book shares real-life tax scenarios and stories collected by the author over years of working directly with clients to help them resolve their tax issues. They are meant to provide generalized examples of what may or may not occur in certain tax-related situations. In order to protect client privacy and anonymity, certain details about such examples have been omitted or altered.

CONTENTS

INTRODUCTION

A universal truth exists in this world that we just can't avoid, no matter how hard some of us might try: Bad things happen to good people.

Now, I'm not saying that bad things *will* happen to you; however, despite our own best efforts, sometimes things just don't work out the way we want them to. Most decisions are made with the best of intentions, but sadly, we can never really know how things will turn out until it's too late. Furthermore, the decisions we make are shaped by our own life experiences. But one of the things that best defines each of us in life is how we choose to react to life's challenges.

The truth is, even though we may act with the best of intentions, we all have to live with the results of our decisions, regardless of how they turn out. And sometimes, things go terribly wrong. Let's face it, solving problems of any magnitude is a skill. If one lives a haphazard life, putting out fires as they occur, then the next fire is almost always right around the corner. However, the hallmark of a proactive and productive person is one who can arrange their life affairs properly with practiced knowledge and a careful strategy.

As a New York State Certified Public Accountant and a Certified Tax Resolution Specialist with the American Society of Tax Problem Solvers, I've seen my fair share of seemingly innocent decisions, made by well-meaning individuals, turn out really badly and result in them owing a lot in income taxes. These are individuals who desperately need help solving their issues. But I have found that the tax issues are not actually the core of the problem; they are symptoms of the disorganization and mismanagement of their own personal and/or business affairs.

The Internal Revenue Service (IRS) is the US Treasury's tax collector. It is a huge organization with a lot of rules and regulations regarding how to collect taxes. And for those who aren't familiar with how the tax collection system operates or who the players in that system are, the IRS can be a very scary entity. Let's state it blankly: The IRS is the largest collection agency in America. But owing income taxes is very different than owing credit card debt; there are *very* few instances where the government will accept less than what is owed to them. And this is precisely why I have written this book. It's meant to be the first step in helping you understand how the IRS works, what they are and are *not* allowed to do, and what your rights are.

I've been a student of individual financial behavior patterns for many years. In my experience, individuals with tax problems often have certain similar characteristics and behaviors; often, serious life events precede a tax problem, such as divorce, death, or a job loss or move. When you couple the stress of those events with either poor education or poor coping skills, you wind up with a troubled taxpayer. So this book is also intended to help you recognize and identify your own negative financial behavior patterns. Because the sad truth is, if you don't help yourself, the IRS won't help you either.

While a central goal of this book is to help individuals avoid tax troubles, it is also meant to serve as a primer on how our tax collection system framework operates for troubled taxpayers. It outlines the various collection alternatives the IRS has for them, even when money is *really* tight. This book describes the work I do every day for my clients, but I can't help but wonder where my clients would all be had they been empowered enough to resolve their own issues without the need for a book such as this, without any knowledge or training in this arena. I also can't help but wonder how much better their lives would be had the behaviors and habits that got them into their trouble never existed in the first place.

That's why this book is more than just a "how to fix your tax problems" manual. Tax problems arise because a set of behaviors and decisions that were set in motion with the best of intentions—before any tax was assessed—go horribly wrong. Identifying the root cause of any problem (especially a tax problem) requires thoughtful consideration and reflection. Whether you haven't filed taxes in many years or you owe gobs of money on returns that were already filed, know that that these are symptoms, not problems.

If you see yourself in any of the stories or anecdotes shared in this book, then you're in the right place. They are intended to demonstrate that you are not alone in your struggle to be an upstanding, tax-paying citizen who stays current and pays taxes on time. Know that there is help out there for you, and you are already on your way to seeking it out by reading this book.

On the other hand, this book is *not* meant for anyone who is a tax protester. If you don't believe in the American duty and responsibility of paying taxes and are looking for a way to fight against having to follow those laws, then I suggest you find another book to read. I'm an advocate for complying with and abiding by the laws of our country. The privilege of living in a place as great as the United States of America comes with trade-offs, as all great privileges in life usually do. In the words of Justice Oliver Wendell Holmes, "Taxes are the price we pay for a civilized society. Taxes are the price we pay for civilization. I like to pay taxes; with them

I buy civilization."[1] The payment of taxes allows the citizens of this country to collectively enjoy the use of those taxes, which in turn improves our standard of living.

That's not to say the system isn't flawed. The tax collection system in the United States is in serious jeopardy. Years of political juggling has left the IRS underfunded, in spite of executing a herculean task of collection the taxes of the nation. Despite recent legislation, the IRS has had a long history of congressional underfunding. These tight purse strings have left the IRS to operate with bandages and twine. Their outdated computer hardware is running outdated computer software. A large percentage of their workforce needs to be replaced over the next decade due to retirements. Most importantly, there are those on the front lines of the collection system who make collection decisions against the taxpaying public arbitrarily, capriciously, and without a sound basis in tax law.

Only an education in your rights and responsibilities can prevent the IRS from behaving outside their legislated scope and protect you from any abuses of discretion. There is an industry truism that "every tax problem has a resolution." This applies to tax-paying citizens as well as to the IRS. My role as a tax problem resolver is to bridge the gap between a tax debtor and a creditor in a way that conforms to the

---

1   Compañia General de Tobacos de Filipinas v. Collector of Internal Revenue, 275 U.S. 87 (1927).

IRS's rules and regulations *and* is respectful of the rights of tax-paying citizens.

Everyone deserves a fair shake when it comes to trying to resolve their tax debt. Regardless of your station in life and the struggles you may be facing, hard decisions have to be made about your financial life when facing the IRS. Simply put, the IRS requires only two things from the tax-paying public: compliance and payment. By reading this book, you are making your first behavior modification, a step toward improving your financial life. My hope is that by its end, you will realize the power of knowing how the IRS works and how to use their system in your favor so that you can return to your life without fear and doubt about what the IRS will do next.

PART I

THE TROUBLE WITH TAXES

CHAPTER 1
Who Is the IRS and Why Should I Care?

When it comes to battle, people say, "know thy enemy," and there's a good reason for it. Knowing who you're up against gives you that much more strength to successfully compete against them. Now, I don't necessarily go around calling the IRS the "enemy," but when it comes to facing tax trouble, they are your biggest adversary on the path to resolving that trouble. They're the opponent who you need to adequately understand and size up if you're going to step into the ring with them and come out largely intact at the end of the match. So you really should get to know them and how they operate.

It all starts with first understanding what taxes are and why there's a system in place that requires us to pay them. Taxes are meant to help provide revenue for federal, state, and local governments so they can fund essential services provided to the public. For example, the taxes we pay are used to help pay for things like building and maintaining highways, funding military defense, and paying the salaries of government employees. The general idea is that a portion of our salaries and other types of earned income are contributed to the government in order to benefit everyone in a variety of ways.

The creation of the US Department of the Treasury, the IRS's governing body, occurred with the ratification of the US Constitution in 1789. It gave the federal government new, stronger powers to tax citizens directly. The taxes were in the form of tariffs and excise taxes. These taxes were used to repay the country's war debt as well as to revitalize the nation's economy after the war. The goal of the tax system was to balance the needs of raising tax revenue against shaping taxpayers' saving and spending habits and the desire to have a fair system.

During the Civil War, the federal government required much more revenue than the tariffs and excise taxes could provide. A tax on income was established in 1862 but was later abolished after the war. The ratification of the Sixteenth Amendment in 1913 gave Congress the right to levy and collect income taxes.

Prior to the ratification of the Sixteenth Amendment, taxes were levied on the population and were known as "poll taxes," as originally written in the US Constitution.

The novelty of the new law is that it levied an income tax on individual and corporate income. The Bureau of Internal Revenue, as it was then known, established a Personal Income Tax Division (assessment and collection), Correspondence Unit (enforcement), and General Counsel (legal opinions).

Under the new law, income taxes were to be self-assessed, and collection was the responsibility of the individual taxpayer to remit to the government. This method of tax administration led to a high level of noncompliance and nonpayment. This legislation marked a departure from previous collection methods, moving away from tariffs and duties and toward the assessment of income taxes.

The first income tax form

The first income tax form (Form 1040) was issued on January 5, 1914. It was a four-page form (including instructions) that taxpayers were instructed to remit with no payments, as field agents were tasked with verifying information and then sending out and collecting tax bills. To further enhance public awareness, the Bureau of Internal Revenue launched a special nationwide public education program to help citizens understand the new income tax. It coincided with the occurrence of World War I. The campaign tried to popularize war taxes by emphasizing the needs of the country and appealing to national pride and patriotism.

The Great Depression brought the care of the elderly, industrial accident victims, unemployed individuals, and people with certain disabilities under federal jurisdiction with the passage of the Social Security Act of 1935. This act required employers to withhold certain monies earmarked for federal benefit programs.

The concept of wage withholding was expanded in 1943 with the Current Tax Payment Act. This act compelled employers to withhold federal income tax from workers' paychecks and pay them directly to the government on the workers' behalf.

Under President Truman, the Bureau of Internal Revenue was reorganized and renamed the Internal Revenue Service on July 9, 1953. The Department of the Treasury was organized with the following bureaus under its full or partial jurisdiction:

- Alcohol and Tobacco Tax and Trade Bureau
- Bureau of Engraving and Printing
- Financial Crimes Enforcement Network
- Bureau of the Fiscal Service
- Office of the Comptroller of the Currency
- Office of the Inspector General
- Treasury Inspector General for Tax Administration
- Special Inspector General for Pandemic Recovery
- Financial Management Service
- United States Mint
- Bureau of the Public Debt
- Office of Thrift Supervision
- Internal Revenue Service

In 1988, the IRS published Publication 1, *Your Rights as a Taxpayer*, an IRS-required disclosure communication to taxpayers. It outlines the taxpayers' rights regarding tax examination, appeal, collection, and refunds. Further improvements and upgrades occurred with the Restructuring and Reform Act of 1998. The IRS Restructuring and Reform Act of 1998 prompted the most comprehensive reorganization and modernization of the IRS in nearly half a century. The IRS reorganized itself in 2000 to closely resemble the private sector, creating four major business divisions, each aligned to a group of taxpayers with similar needs.

Herein lies the largest issue with the IRS today: It is treated like Congress's stepchild when it comes to funding the tax collection process. The legislature continually bootstraps the agency, leaving the tax collection operations of the federal government to remain consistently understaffed and working with a patchwork of overlapping and asynchronous technologies that are fifty or sixty years old. Think about that for a moment. Can you imagine trying to efficiently accomplish *anything* in your life today by using outdated technology? Neither can I.

The Taxpayer Advocate Service, an independent organization within the IRS, submits their report on the state of the IRS to Congress every year. In the 2022 report, Erin Collins, the head of the Taxpayer Advocate Service, highlighted some of the more serious problems at the IRS: processing delays of paper returns, weaknesses in human capital acquisition and training, and online access for taxpayers and tax professionals.[2]

Despite recent increased allocations to fund the IRS, they are not nearly enough to fix a broken system. Most of

---

2   "Full Report." 2024. Taxpayer Advocate Service. June 26, 2024. https://www.taxpayeradvocate.irs.gov/reports/2025-objectives-report-to-congress/full-report/.

the 87,000 agents the IRS has scheduled for hire over the next ten years are mainly to replace an aging and retiring workforce. The tax collection system in this country is broken. And we, as tax-paying citizens, are paying the price via delayed refunds to taxpayers, extended processing delays due to workforce needs within the IRS, and poor telephone customer service.

It's no wonder the IRS is the scariest collection agency on the planet, when 85 percent of the national budget is funded by your paycheck tax withholding and estimated income tax payments. Worse off, they have the legal right to collect every penny they say you owe them. This is why it's so important for you, as the taxpayer, to understand what the IRS legally can and can't do and what your rights are, to make sure those boundaries are clearly defined.

And yet it can be extremely difficult to understand how the tax collection system works, what your rights are within it, and how you're even supposed to keep yourself out of trouble, let alone get yourself out of trouble when you land in it. This is due in part to the IRS making their processes a veritable rat maze to navigate. You can see evidence of what I mean in their "Taxpayer Roadmap Tool," a public graphic you can find on their website.[3]

---

3   https://www.taxpayeradvocate.irs.gov/get-help/roadmap/

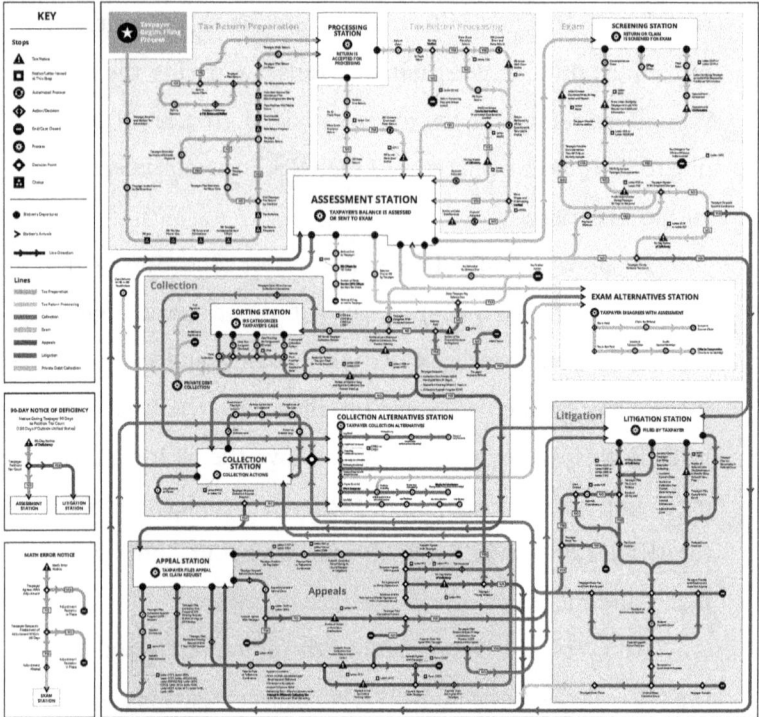

This "roadmap" is meant to "help" taxpayers better understand how the collection system works. Instead, it's an absolutely dizzying display of confusing information that even I, as a tax resolution professional, have trouble making heads or tails of. Looking at it as an average American taxpayer, it looks more complicated than a New York City subway map. *That* is the line of thinking you're up against when it comes to the IRS. They've taken it upon themselves to throw information at you in any way they please, then leave it up to you to detangle and interpret. And that's why people who smell smoke often end up with a full-blown fire on their hands. They don't understand what their options are within the IRS's laws and systems.

Now, the IRS is our country's most formidable collection agency, responsible for enforcing tax laws and collecting taxes owed to the government. Its tax collection process is described as methodical and unwavering, designed to ensure compliance with those same tax laws. From initial notifications to more severe measures like liens, levies, and garnishments, the IRS employs a systematic approach designed to enforce compliance. The book emphasizes that tax issues stem from deeper behavioral and financial management problems rather than the tax debt itself. The IRS has extensive legal authority to collect taxes, so understanding this process is crucial for the protection of taxpayers' rights and navigating out of tax trouble. By knowing how the system works and recognizing their own financial behaviors, taxpayers can proactively resolve their issues and avoid future complications.

CHAPTER 2
What Is Wrong with Our Taxes

Our tax system is a "voluntary" one only to the extent that taxes should be voluntarily reported and remitted to the government rather than not doing so and facing forced seizure or forfeiture of assets, or worse, prosecution for tax offenses. So when it comes to income taxes, the IRS only wants two simple things from every tax-paying citizen: to file one's tax return on time, and to pay what's due. That's it. If you consistently do both of those things correctly, the IRS will generally leave you alone.

When either one of those two requirements is ignored by a taxpayer, that's when the IRS reacts. And unfortunately, the IRS really doesn't care what reason you had for not filing your returns or paying your taxes on time, they just want the taxes due from the income you voluntarily reported and are now required to pay.

The problem with taxes is, you don't get the same enjoyment and satisfaction from paying your taxes as you would from paying for any other good or service. Despite that, for most of us, earning our living and paying our taxes is the price of admission in a civilized society. But then, inexplicably, there are those of us who, for whatever reason, can't seem to get it together. Those citizens face dealing with this agency, whose job is to assess and collect taxes, with seemingly very little regard for personal circumstances.

A prime example that highlights the problem with taxes begins with the story of a client of a colleague of mine, an older gentleman who decided, after many years of not filing his taxes, to prepare his own returns. And each return he prepared claimed a significant refund on the return, so this taxpayer thought he would be able to retire on all the refunds claimed for each return filed. His refund claims from all the delinquent income tax returns totaled about $500,000. Thinking a big payday was on the way, the taxpayer finally filed his returns—and was only able to recover $1,500 of the $500,000 claimed. What he failed to realize is that the IRS has a rule that restricts your ability to defer the filing of a tax return, even if you are owed a refund. The lesson here is to always file your tax return on time, *especially when you are due a refund.*

So, for those of us who can't seem to get it together, the annual task of filing and paying taxes can be the most difficult and confusing financial decision one makes. And for many of us, it simply comes down to a lack of understanding and/or an inability to follow our tax reporting and collection system. We all live very intricate and complicated financial lives, and staying in the IRS's good graces can be very challenging.

My role as a tax resolution specialist is to assist taxpayers in getting right with the IRS and set them on a better path than they were on previously. When someone decides to fix their tax issue and hire me, they have to be ready, willing, and able to fix the problem and *change their habits* so that it doesn't happen again. Now, it is understandable that there will be bumps along the way, but making changes to one's lifestyle is always difficult.

It is easy to just say that bad things happen to good people, but when you are blind to the source of your problems, or more often than not, *you* are the source, that's a different story altogether. Filing and paying one's taxes is a social responsibility one should take very seriously. And for those who need it, there is competent and professional help available. Honest mistakes are all well and good once in a while, but if trouble seems to find you more often than not, it's something that needs to be looked at more closely.

Taxpayers I've worked with, who have gotten into trouble in one way or another, are generally remorseful about the errors of their ways. Together, we formulate the necessary steps to correct those errors and create safeguards to make sure the problem doesn't reoccur. These are the same people who seem to always make bad business decisions or have poor spending habits; they can't seem to get out of their own way. But we must be willing to take responsibility into our own hands. Because once again, the IRS won't take on that responsibility for you. Their only responsibility is to the US government.

I believe that there's a resolution to every tax situation. It may not always be a resolution that the taxpayer is completely happy about, but it will be one that brings things to a final conclusion after all the fear, misunderstanding, and stress you've been experiencing. And in the end, that's really the goal—to get your life back to a place where you can finally start rebuilding it without the threat of the proverbial 800-pound tax-collection gorilla standing over you.

PART II

HOW THE TAX SYSTEM WORKS

CHAPTER 3
Taxpayer Responsibilities vs. IRS Responsibilities

As mentioned in the previous chapter, it's our responsibility as working American citizens to pay the taxes we owe to the US government each year on time and in full. You can achieve that in a variety of ways, depending on what your income looks like, whether it's through withholding from your employer, sending estimated tax payments every quarter, or if you're a business owner with employees on a payroll, making sure those taxes make their way to the government as required. There are also taxes due for things that aren't directly related to your income, such as paying monthly property taxes on the house you own.

Because there are so many different taxes you can be required to pay, depending on your situation, the best way to think of it is this: Any type of remuneration—wages, interest, dividends, or any other type of compensation you receive—counts as taxable income that you must report. There are always exceptions, of course, but we'll get into some of those later on as they become relevant.

If you work with a certified public accountant (CPA), they'll figure out what all your taxable income looks like and what you owe on it. If you file your taxes yourself, it's up to you to figure out how to file them correctly. You can lean on services like TurboTax for guidance, but even their systems are based on automated templates and categories that aren't always one-size-fits-all. This is why I urge people to make an effort to clearly understand what they owe, why they owe it, when they owe it, and how to pay it. Even so, if you file your own taxes and during your attempt to file correctly you make some kind of mistake, the IRS does allow you to correct it. There is a process for that situation. And again, it's all because it is every American's responsibility to timely file and pay their income taxes.

Paying one's fair share of taxes is one of those civic responsibilities we take on in order to contribute to the well-being of our local and national communities. It's similar to voting in elections and reporting for jury duty. However, the fact remains that many of us fail to make the choice to timely file and pay our income taxes. In fact, the tale of a troubled taxpayer begins with a plan that seems like a good idea in the moment but winds up causing more problems than it solves.

For example, think about the taxpayer who decides, for whatever reason, to not file a tax return. That strategy would be all well and good if you live in extreme poverty. But when you've left a trail of earned income over a span of six, seven, or eight years, the IRS *will* take notice. And the longer the acts of noncompliance linger, the worse the problem becomes.

In response to this civic responsibility failure by the taxpayer, the IRS starts sending notice after notice to obtain a tax return from the delinquent filer. The IRS gives taxpayers opportunity after opportunity to submit a tax return before they decide to take action.

Civic responsibility takes a further hit when taxpayers continue to ignore the "failure to file" letters from the IRS. That's when the IRS exercises its own brand of civic responsibility (backed by the law of the land) by beginning the process of *filing your tax return for you.* Trust me when I tell you, this is not a service you want performed by the IRS. They will apply the highest tax rate on your income, deny you any of the deductions you are legally entitled to, and to add insult to injury, apply penalties and interest to the amounts owed and the act of failure to file.

The truth is, abdicating your civic responsibility to file and pay your taxes could land you in jail. Civil remedies include penalties and interest; criminal penalties for tax evasion or fraud include jail time. But before the IRS wastes time on incarcerating citizens, they will deploy a variety of other strategies to get taxpayers to fulfill their civic responsibility, all in the name of tax collection.

Substitute for Return

An IRS Substitute for Return (SFR) is a tax return prepared by the IRS on behalf of the delinquent filer in order to assess an income tax against the taxpayer. The assessment is based on information the IRS has in its wage and income transcripts that are reported by third parties such as employers, banks, and financial institutions.

An SFR is not the same as a taxpayer-filed return. An SFR is an internal document used to quantify the amount of tax owed by the taxpayer. Taxes are calculated at the highest possible rate and many exemptions, deductions, and credits are restricted or denied, compared to a taxpayer-filed return. More important are the penalties and interest the IRS is allowed to assess against the non-filer.

While the SFR is being prepared, the IRS will send out a stream of notices to grab the taxpayer's attention on the issue. The last notice, known as a Notice of Deficiency, is a legally binding notice that informs the taxpayer of the assessment and their right to appeal the determination.

If you think something is amiss with the notice letters the IRS is sending you, or you do not have the ability to do what they're asking you to do, you have two options:

1) Learn and then take the necessary actions you're able to take on your own behalf, or 2) reach out to a tax resolution professional to do the heavy (and often confusing) lifting for you. My business, The Tax Relief Pro, is one such professional service you could reach out to. And though someone such as I can help you navigate the waters you're treading, it doesn't mean you should stop reading this book right here and now. That's because this book is meant to help you better understand the actions we can take together to figure your situation out. And when you better understand what your options are, you'll have more confidence in navigating them and understanding how they might affect you.

Whether you are capable of paying in full or not, the next step will be to explore alternate resolution options and possibly appeal options if necessary. If you don't take any such action, the IRS will begin employing the use of enforced collections to attempt to gather what's owed to them. They have a variety of strategies and tactics to collect taxes owed, including:

- Federal tax liens
- Bank levies
- Wage garnishments
- Federal payment offset
- Passport revocation
- Asset seizures
- Installment agreements
- Offers in compromise
- Civil and criminal penalties
- Judgments

Several of the remaining chapters in this book will go into further detail about what each of the above is, when they come into play, and what your options are when faced with the possibility of one or more of them occurring. But before they do, it's important to first understand what kind of timelines the IRS must abide by in their tax administration function and how those timelines may be used to your advantage in some cases.

CHAPTER 4
CSED, ASED, and RSED: What Are They and Why Should I Care?

The law provides three distinct periods of time to review, analyze, and resolve issues with a taxpayer's account(s) of record. These laws are known as "statutes of limitation." They define the time allowed for the IRS to assess tax liability, collect taxes, or act on a refund claim. Each of these periods has its own significance, purpose, and method of calculation, and each of them has its own deadline after which the IRS can no longer act.

The collection statute defines the maximum period during which the IRS can legally pursue the collection of unpaid taxes from the taxpayer. On the collection statute expiration date (CSED), the IRS loses the legal authority to collect the outstanding tax debt. The CSED is generally ten years from the date of the assessment. Sadly though, troubled taxpayers are often troubled financially as well. They often create their own "tolling events," or events that pause the CSED from expiring. These are events like requesting an installment agreement, filing bankruptcy, or submitting an offer in compromise, which all extend the time the IRS has to fully collect all the taxes, penalties, and interest assessed.

Calculating CSEDs is not an easy task. The IRS has an arsenal of tax, penalty, and interest assessments that can be posted to a tax account, or "IRS module," as it is known. And if there are multiple years of unpaid taxes that need to be resolved, the calculations become unwieldy. Moreover, in any given tax "module," there is no limit as to how many assessments can be made. There could be multiple assessments of tax, penalty, and/or interest, each one having its own assessment date.

Knowing where you stand in the IRS collection queue is a critical piece of information. Here is an example of a collection case falling through the cracks. I have a client who started out with me over ten years ago with $250,000 in tax debt. At the time, the taxpayer's passport had been certified as a delinquent taxpayer, restricting her ability to travel, which she was required to do for work. After examining her transcripts, I also noticed a CSED mistake which, when fixed, reduced the overstated collection statute by five years. Her original amount due to the IRS was nearly a quarter million dollars, with penalties and interest. After fixing the passport issue, the IRS never followed up with collection notices. The IRS's collection inaction has now reduced the taxpayer's debt to about $100,000 due to expiration of the collection statute.

One last important word on CSEDs, for all of those "wait and see" taxpayers who cause their own troubles by not filing their income taxes: The IRS has a tax-filing mechanism for those who decide not to file their own return, and that is the substitute for return (SFR). An SFR is determined by the IRS for the sole purpose of collecting income taxes. The SFR for a return filed by the IRS on behalf of the taxpayer is not the same as it would be for a return voluntarily filed by the taxpayer. This mechanism is intended to weed out the non-filing taxpayers.

The assessment statute expiration date (ASED) marks the last date on which the IRS can make any assessments of tax, penalty, and/or interest for any given tax year. A voluntarily filed income tax return automatically starts the three-year period during which the IRS can propose any changes of tax and/or impose any penalties and/or interest on a tax account. The ASED does not start until an original income tax return is filed by the taxpayer, as the IRS is unable to establish appropriate collection or refund eligibility dates without a taxpayer-filed return. Due to the large inventory of known unfiled returns by "high-income" non-filers (defined by the IRS as people who report greater than $100,000 of adjusted gross income), there is a concerted effort at the IRS to have delinquent returns filed and taxes paid (plus penalties and interest) by the responsible taxpayers.

The refund statute expiration date (RSED) is the deadline for claiming a tax refund from the IRS. In other words, the IRS is not legally bound to refund any income tax overpayments voluntarily. Claims for refunds must be submitted to the IRS in writing, three years from the original due date of the return or two years from the date the tax was paid, whichever is later. Missing the RSED means the taxpayer loses any right to receive the refund they are owed.

This reminds me of a soon-to-be divorcing couple who had, in retrospect, not hired the most competent tax preparer. This particular preparer added to the taxpayers' tax problems by failing to timely transmit the taxpayer's 2018 income tax return, which claimed a sizable refund. This was only discovered by a careful analysis of their transcripts as part of an overall tax resolution plan. Once I informed the taxpayers of this deficiency, a return was filed. However, since the RSED had come and gone, the taxpayers forfeited an $18,000 federal income tax refund. It is essential to file your tax return and claim any eligible refunds in a timely manner.

Understanding these dates is crucial for managing income tax debt effectively. The collection statute can provide the necessary information about knowing when the IRS's collection efforts become limited and when those limits expire. Tracking income tax penalties and associated interest are dependent upon the timing of each assessment, as outlined in the assessment statute, while the refund statute ensures that you don't miss out on potential refunds that may be used to offset existing debt. Having the right professional tax resolution representation is critical to navigating these dates and developing a tax resolution strategy based on your specific circumstances.

CHAPTER 5
Enforced Collections

The majority of American citizens fulfill their tax obligations in a timely manner. However, there are instances where an individual or business finds themselves unable to pay their income taxes. Enforced collections is the process by which the IRS collects unpaid taxes.

Since enforced collections is a structured process designed to give the taxpayer every opportunity to address the tax liabilities, it should not be taken lightly. Most often, because of the tax debt owed, the IRS files a lien when proposing just about any type of installment agreement. This is to protect the government's interests and ability to collect the outstanding tax debt over the collection statute. Liens are effective against taxpayers who own valuables such as homes, boats, motorcycles, artwork, or collectibles.

Simply put, when an individual or business fails to file and/or pay their income taxes, the IRS has the power to file the return for you and collect the tax liability plus penalties and interest. Before the IRS can begin enforced collection actions, such as levying a taxpayer's bank account or garnishing wages, they must follow a series of legally required steps. These steps include sending specific notices to the taxpayer, ensuring that they are informed of the debt and are provided with opportunities to resolve the issue.

Once such notice, the statutory notice of deficiency (SNOD), is a critical notice in the tax resolution process. While not a collection notice per se, it informs the taxpayer of the additional actions the IRS intends to take if the tax debt remains uncollected. It also provides a ninety-day window in which to dispute the proposed assessment in tax court.

Each of the IRS's required delinquency notices communicates the type of deficiency the taxpayer has, why the taxpayer is receiving this final notice, and what their rights as a taxpayer are. They play a crucial role in the collection process, ensuring that taxpayers are adequately informed and given opportunities to address their tax liabilities before the IRS takes enforced collection actions. Understanding these notices and responding appropriately can help taxpayers avoid more severe consequences.

One of my first tax resolution clients, whose $65,000 of debt was resolved for $1,500 dollars, is the perfect example. When I first started my practice, I made a house call to an elderly couple who had received a series of collection notices from the IRS for tax returns that had gone unfiled for quite some time. When I questioned the taxpayers about why the returns hadn't been filed, they said they had been advised not to file by their now-deceased tax preparer. Bad advice aside, the IRS identified a potential source of tax revenue and sent the taxpayers all sorts of collections letters. In the pile of unopened mail, I found the SNOD I needed to resolve their tax debt.

Should the taxpayer still not demonstrate a willingness to resolve their tax debt, the IRS has more tools available in its collection arsenal to recover delinquent income taxes, other than just mailing collection letters. The IRS has the authority to seize assets and property when an individual or business fails to meet their tax obligations. The following is a descriptive list of the tools they use.

Liens: Most people are unaware that filing a tax return with a balance due creates a "secret" lien, or a lien that is not apparent or publicly known to any parties, especially creditors. To protect and perfect its collection interests, the IRS may issue a notice of federal tax lien in the county of the taxpayer's residence to secure its position for repayment. Liens are generally attached to the taxpayer's property (real or personal) *and* any subsequently owned property at the time the lien is issued. Having a federal income tax lien may affect your creditworthiness or employability. The IRS notifies taxpayers by sending copies of the lien filings to the taxpayer's last known address by certified US mail, as required by law.

The general threshold for the automatic filing of a federal income tax lien is $10,000 of tax debt. There are several ways in which a lien may be removed. The primary method of releasing a lien is to pay the debt in full, either in a lump sum or in an installment agreement. There are circumstances in which a taxpayer may have the lien withdrawn due to an IRS error in issuing the lien, such as issuing it to the wrong party. Liens may also be subrogated, meaning that the IRS allows another creditor ahead of the IRS in order to facilitate IRS collection of overdue taxes.

Levies: A levy is a collection activity used by the IRS to forcibly satisfy an income tax debt without having to go to court. A levy only captures property possessed by the debtor at the time the levy is served, which is different than the filing of a lien, which attaches to all owned and "after acquired" property.

A levy may occur when all the following three events occur:

1. The IRS sends the legally required notice and demand for payment of taxes.

2. The taxpayer fails to pay within ten days of the letter (known as a "10-day letter").

3. The IRS must give the taxpayer notice of the right to a hearing thirty days before the levy takes place (known as a "30-day letter").

Ken, a business development colleague of mine and a fellow business owner, enlisted my help with a levy notice he received from the IRS. Ken is a subcontractor to Bob, another business owner, so Bob pays Ken for his services. In their capacity to collect Ken's income tax debt, the IRS sent a collection notice to one of his customers—in this case, Bob. Could you imagine how embarrassed Ken must have been when Bob showed him the levy notice? Thankfully, Bob didn't owe Ken any money, otherwise he would have had to turn it over to the IRS instead.

Garnishments: A garnishment is a continuous levy based on a fixed and determinable series of payments. This tactic is typically used with troubled taxpayers who earn wages. To enforce a garnishment, the IRS issues a notice of garnishment to the debtor's employer, and the employer is then required to impound funds from the wages and remit the garnished amounts. Since garnishments are a continuous type of levy, they are extinguished when the total tax debt is paid. Wage earners who owe the IRS taxes could lose up to 85 percent of their take-home pay as the result of a garnishment.

Levies and garnishments are employed when the taxpayer has not responded to previous collection notifications. If the debt goes unpaid, the IRS serves the taxpayer's financial institution and/or custodian with a levy notice. This includes banks, investment accounts, retirement accounts, the cash value of life insurance, business receivables, and trust distributions; all are fair game if you owe income taxes.

Imagine for a moment that you are another former client of mine, who we'll call Roger. Roger just got out of bankruptcy and owes the IRS approximately $225,000. He has no assets, was recently divorced, and is the father of three grown children who he is still supporting. What further complicates Roger's ability to pay his tax debts is that he is living paycheck to paycheck as a salaried salesperson. The IRS will not accept his installment agreement request because the amount that Roger wanted to pay was less than the legally enforceable wage levy issued by the IRS. You don't want to be in the same tough position Roger is in.

Federal Payment Offset: The Treasury Offset Program is designed to collect a variety of delinquent debts, including income taxes. Under the program, certain payments to a debtor could be intercepted if you owe income taxes, including tax refunds, Social Security benefits, federal student loans, and federal wage and salary payments.

Asset Seizure: In cases of significant tax debt, the IRS will seize property and sell it to satisfy tax debts. This can include homes, cars, boats, jewelry, and other personal property. If the object to be seized is moveable, the IRS takes physical possession of it. Otherwise, an IRS revenue officer "tags" the property by padlocking it. IRS asset seizures are also keeping up with technology and the internet. It is easy to imagine the IRS tagging and seizing houses, cars, jewelry, and even farm animals to satisfy an outstanding tax debt. They've stepped up their game in their ability to track down hidden electronic assets too, such as cryptocurrency.

For those who may not know, cryptocurrency is an electronic medium of exchange that exists only on the internet. It has been the source of many financial scams and dodges. One such electronic marketplace known as the Silk Road was the source of a $1 billion asset forfeiture by the US Department of Justice in 2020, based on a criminal investigation carried out by the IRS.

All real, tangible, and intangible property held by the debtor taxpayer may be subject to levy or seizure.

Passport Revocation: The IRS can also alert the justice department regarding your tax debt if it exceeds $62,000 (the figure for 2024, which is adjusted each year for inflation). That is the threshold by which the IRS considers tax debt "seriously delinquent" enough so as to restrict the issuance of a travel passport. Taxpayers who have their travel privileges revoked must contact the IRS, pay the debt, or make payment arrangements in order to have the certification reversed. The justice department will then suspend the passport application for ninety days or until notified by the IRS of the debt satisfaction.

As we've explored in the previous chapters, the IRS has an arsenal of tools and strategies for enforcing tax collections, which can feel overwhelming and intimidating. Understanding these methods is crucial, but knowing that there are viable pathways to resolution is equally important.

Now that we have a clear picture of what the IRS can do, it's time to shift our focus to the options available to you. In the next section, we will dive into the various resolution strategies that exist and how to assert your rights if you disagree with any IRS action. Let's explore these areas and how they can be tailored to your specific situation.

PART III

YOUR TAX
RESOLUTION OPTIONS

CHAPTER 6
Payment Arrangements

It is critical to recognize the importance of addressing past due taxes promptly. Ignoring your tax obligations can lead to severe consequences, as described in the previous chapter. The IRS is the nation's most powerful creditor; they possess a broad authority to collect what is owed to them. Taking proactive steps to resolve your tax debt not only helps you avoid additional penalties and/or interest, but it also provides peace of mind and a clear path to financial stability.

The IRS offers several programs designed to assist delinquent taxpayers with fulfilling their tax obligations in a manageable way. However, any IRS payment arrangement is contingent upon the taxpayer achieving filing compliance. The mission-critical element of any payment arrangement sought with the IRS is having all your income tax returns filed. Filing delinquent returns is the first "good-faith" effort a taxpayer can make in getting current with their tax obligations.

The IRS offers a short menu of payment arrangement options to accommodate different financial situations once a final tax bill is assessed. They may mandate the submission of financial information in order to evaluate the taxpayer's ability to repay their tax debts over a prescribed period of time, but not longer than the collection statute allows (as explained in Chapter 4).

The IRS's financial evaluation begins by calculating the taxpayer's reasonable collection potential, or the amount of money the IRS believes it can collect from the taxpayer's monthly disposable income and equity in assets. In short, what the IRS wants to know is 1) how much of your monthly disposable income they can take and 2) the liquidation value of your home, automobiles, and any other valuables you may own.

After collecting all the taxpayer's financial data, they apply certain analytical tools to assess each taxpayer's ability to pay without creating an undue hardship to the taxpayer. These tools, known as "collection standards," measure the taxpayer's monthly disposable income and equity in assets in order to determine the payment arrangement most favorable to the IRS.

There are several types of payment plans that may then be utilized.

Installment Agreement: This plan allows taxpayers to pay their tax debts, including interest and penalties, over an extended period of time. Terms can be as short as six months or as long as is allowed by the CSED. In this type of arrangement, the IRS would receive all the taxes owed.

Partial Payment Installment Agreement: This plan is very similar to an installment agreement, but the amount collected according to the collection statute will not satisfy the entire tax debt, hence the name. As the name suggests, it usually implies that there is a special circumstance that prevents a taxpayer from repaying the whole tax obligation. Sometimes a pre-existing health condition or unusual financial stress affects the taxpayer's ability to generate enough income to pay some of the debt.

Offer in Compromise: This plan allows taxpayers to settle their tax debt for less than the full amount owed, providing one qualifies for this type of option. While the results of an offer in compromise may be similar to a partial pay installment agreement (paying less than the total amount owed), the main difference is that an offer in compromise is a legally binding contract between the debtor and the IRS. Installment agreements can be initiated, modified, defaulted on, and restarted once again. An offer in compromise brings total finality to the tax debtor.

Currently Not Collectible: This plan temporarily halts collection activities if the taxpayer can demonstrate that paying the debt would cause significant economic hardship. This is best illustrated by a client of mine named Scott, a divorced man in his early fifties, the father of four adult children, who has kidney disease. His pension and Social Security are his only sources of income and are being used for his health and welfare. He is able to demonstrate that his illness prevents him from paying the IRS anything now and throughout the term outlined by the collection statute, because covering the costs of his illness supersedes the IRS's ability to collect. That is an added benefit of this type of arrangement: It allows the collection statute to run its course.

Most installment agreement requests require some type of financial disclosure by the taxpayer, signed under penalty of perjury, to make sure they obtain the correct payment arrangement. Often this will necessitate the submission of proof of income (including pay stubs), bank and investment statements, a listing of household expenses, and any legally binding debt obligations, such as mortgages. Each taxpayer's financial information is compared to the IRS standards to arrive at a repayment amount.

This is when having a tax resolution specialist can be particularly helpful in this process. The IRS will likely provide you with a payment arrangement which favors full tax collection without regard to your financial situation. A certified tax resolution specialist can help you obtain your financial freedom with a properly structured payment arrangement that you can realistically uphold.

And, in the event that one is unable to come to terms with the IRS and their overdue taxes, taxpayers have the right to elevate their concerns both within and outside the IRS so that they receive fair and just treatment under the law. That is done through the appeals process, the topic of the next chapter.

CHAPTER 7
The Appeals Process

The IRS established the Independent Office of Appeals for those instances when a taxpayer and the IRS can't agree on a solution to the taxpayer's issues, whether it's about a tax examination or a collection issue. The Office of Appeals' primary purpose is to resolve tax disputes without litigation. It provides an opportunity to settle disagreements over tax assessments, penalties, and other tax-related issues in an efficient and impartial manner. By offering an alternative to the formal court system, the Office of Appeals helps to streamline the resolution process, saving time and resources for both the taxpayer and the government.

There are typically two sources of controversy that can be handled by the Independent Office of Appeals. An appeal usually starts as the result of some type of adverse tax audit, examination, or collection action that the taxpayer disagrees with. The types of appeal available to the taxpayer to challenge an action or proposed action by the IRS are either a collection due process hearing or a collection appeals program hearing. The type of appeal used will depend on the taxpayer's specific situation and issue to be resolved.

A Collection Appeals Program (CAP) hearing differs from a collection due process (CDP) hearing in that it is purely an administrative hearing that provides the taxpayer with a way to question an alleged unpaid tax. In establishing the program in 1996, the IRS allows the taxpayer to challenge 1) the proposed filing or the actual filing of a federal income tax lien, 2) the denial, rejection, modification, or termination of any installment agreement, or 3) the serving of a levy.

Generally speaking, a taxpayer is allowed to request a conference when they disagree with a collection decision or action taken by an IRS revenue officer. The purpose of the managerial conference is to review the case and attempt to resolve disputes without escalating to more formal appeals processes or litigation.

During the conference, the taxpayer or their representative can present additional information, clarify misunderstandings, and negotiate terms related to collection activities, such as installment agreements, offers in compromise, or the release of liens. The manager has the authority to override or modify the decisions made by the revenue officers, aiming to ensure the fair and equitable treatment of the taxpayer while still pursuing the collection of taxes owed.

For instance, a revenue officer I worked with some time ago proposed a levy on my client Peter's paycheck as a matter of resolving his tax debt. But the revenue officer and I disagreed on how much the taxpayer could afford to pay, as stated on the collection information statement. Since we were unable to agree on a final payment amount, I filed for a managerial conference as an appeal to resolve the matter.

The CAP offers an immediate forum for taxpayers to challenge collection actions with a fair, impartial, and expedited process. This "rapid review" process ensures that disputes are addressed before any further harmful actions, like levies and seizures, are executed. My client Susie owed over $250,000 in income taxes and wanted the IRS to terminate a bank levy because it was creating an economic hardship for her. By filing an appeal, she was provided a forum for a fair, impartial, and timely review of the matter, and her request was eventually granted. The CAP excludes appeals emanating primarily from a trust fund recovery assessment, rejection of an offer in compromise, and penalty assessments. Lastly and most importantly, any decision by the IRS during a collection appeal is final and binding.

The collection due process (CDP) appeal is a formal hearing aimed at providing taxpayers the right to be heard before the IRS proceeds with certain collection actions (e.g., filing a lien or issuing a levy). This process allows taxpayers to present their case, dispute the validity of the collection action, and propose alternative resolutions, such as an installment agreement or an offer in compromise. The CDP rights in a hearing are not the same as the name might imply. Guarantees of due process *do not* apply to tax collection. The hearings are available to protect taxpayers' rights and to limit IRS collection powers. Added protection is provided by a US Tax Court review.

With a clear understanding of the appeals process and the various avenues available to challenge the IRS, you now have the tools to fight back when the odds seem stacked against you. But while navigating the system is essential, there are special circumstances and advanced strategies that can further safeguard your financial future. As we move into Part IV, we'll delve into these specialized topics, from bankruptcy options to innocent spouse relief, and explore the additional resources that can be critical in resolving even the most complex tax issues. These insights will equip you with the knowledge to make informed decisions and protect your rights in the face of adversity.

PART IV

SPECIAL TOPICS AND RESOURCES

CHAPTER 8
Bankruptcy as a
Resolution Option

One of the biggest myths about income taxes is that they cannot be discharged in a bankruptcy proceeding. The myth is so pervasive and persistent that I often hear attorneys recite it. While bankruptcy is commonly associated with discharging consumer debt, such as credit card balances and/ or medical debt, it can be used for discharging federal income tax debt under the right conditions.

There are benefits and drawbacks to choosing to bankrupt one's income tax debt, so proper planning is mission critical. An elderly couple I worked with some time ago had amassed an incredible amount of tax debts over a series of years mainly due to financial struggles, health issues for both taxpayers, and, the final blow, the national health crisis that resulted from the COVID-19 pandemic, decimating the value of the one asset in their possession: a dental practice.

The one bright spot for these taxpayers was that they filed timely returns each and every year. In spite of their financial woes, they made sure they filed their income tax returns, all as balance due returns. Their pre-bankruptcy income tax debt was approximately $250,000. After preparing a careful analysis of the tax debt using the bankruptcy discharge tests described below, the taxpayers were able to wipe out all but $25,000 dollars, which represented the two most recent tax year filings.

The two most common forms of bankruptcy are a Chapter 7 bankruptcy and a Chapter 13 bankruptcy. The former is known as a liquidation plan, whereby all of the debtor's nonexempt assets are used to pay off creditors. The latter is known a reorganization plan, whereby the debtor is allowed to keep their property and pay debts based on a court-approved repayment plan.

While not all debts are dischargeable in bankruptcy, income tax debt must qualify be discharged in court. In order to qualify for discharge, the income tax debt must pass the following three tests:

1. The income tax debt in question must have been due for at least three years, including extensions, before the filing of the bankruptcy.

2. The income tax return to which the debt applies must have been filed at least two years before the

bankruptcy filing. Depending on the federal court jurisdiction in which you reside, late filed income tax returns may or may not qualify for bankruptcy.

3. The tax debt in question must have been assessed by the IRS at least 240 days before the filing of the bankruptcy.

Bankrupt individuals must submit to the court detailed financial information about their assets, liabilities, and monthly cash flow. The court then determines which debts have a security interest attached to them, such as a house, car, or boat. This means that if the debt isn't satisfied, the seller can seize the property for nonpayment. Unsecured debt is similar to credit card debt, medical debt, overdue bills, and personal loans. This assists the court in determining the priority with which to pay the debtor's creditors, depending on the bankruptcy plan chosen. Priority debts are those debts which must be addressed before any competing claims are considered. Examples include child support, alimony, criminal fines, and federal income taxes.

Wiping out debt of any sort can be a great relief to anyone, as it allows the debtor a fresh start and enables them to focus on future financial planning. While in bankruptcy, any and all income tax collection efforts are suspended until six months after the bankruptcy. Some of the drawbacks to bankruptcy are the complexity and cost of the process, the impact on one's credit, and most importantly, the survival of any pre-bankruptcy income tax liens and nondischarge-able income tax debt. One last complication to consider: If the IRS thinks the debtor has willfully evaded taxes or committed fraud, the IRS could object to the bankruptcy proceeding.

CHAPTER 9
Innocent Spouse

The innocent spouse rules are a crucial aspect of tax resolution, particularly for individuals who find themselves facing joint tax liabilities due to the actions of their spouses. These rules are designed to provide relief to individuals who filed joint tax returns but were unaware of inaccuracies or omissions made by their spouse, which resulted in an understatement of tax. Understanding these rules is vital for those who may be unfairly held liable for their spouse's tax debts.

Eligibility for innocent spouse relief hinges on several critical criteria. Joint and several liability on joint tax returns means that both spouses are equally responsible for the entire tax debt. However, the innocent spouse rules provide three main types of relief:

- innocent spouse relief,
- separation of liability relief,
- equitable relief.

Each type has distinct requirements and is applicable under different circumstances. Innocent spouse relief is available when the spouse was unaware of the understatement of tax. Separation of liability relief is applicable when the couple is divorced, separated, or no longer living together, and the liability is divided between the spouses. Equitable relief is granted when it would be unfair to hold the spouse liable, even if they do not meet the criteria for the other two types of relief.

Innocent spouse relief requires the applicant to meet specific conditions, such as proving they were unaware of the understatement at the time they signed the joint return. The application process involves submitting Form 8857 and providing detailed documentation to support the claim. Common pitfalls include incomplete documentation and missing deadlines, which can be avoided with careful preparation.

Separation of liability relief, on the other hand, is available to divorced or legally separated individuals, or those who have been living apart for at least twelve months. The IRS allocates the tax liability between the spouses based on their respective incomes and responsibilities. This type of relief requires the applicant to demonstrate their eligibility and provide supporting evidence to ensure a fair division of tax liability.

Equitable relief is a last resort for those who do not qualify for the other types of relief but would suffer unfair financial hardship if held liable. The IRS considers various factors, such as the applicant's marital status, economic hardship, and whether they benefited from the understatement. Applying for equitable relief involves submitting Form 8857 and providing a thorough explanation of the circumstances that justify the request.

One such case involved a client of mine, a woman whose husband had left her a bankrupt estate and a mountain of unpaid bills, including a $125,000 income tax debt. I spent hours interviewing the innocent spouse and her daughter so they could recount to me the economic life they lived while she was married to her spouse. The stories of verbal and financial abuse had to be relayed to the IRS with supporting documentation, demonstrating that the taxpayer did not owe the amounts shown on the returns as filed. The taxpayer was able to prove the filed returns were fraudulent. It was heart wrenching to hear her stories, but in the end, the taxpayer prevailed. When I told her that her case was over, she broke down in tears.

The innocent spouse rules offer essential protections for individuals facing joint tax liabilities due to their spouse's actions. Understanding these rules and navigating the application process can be complex, but with the right guidance and preparation, individuals can achieve financial protection and peace of mind. Tax resolution specialists play a crucial role in guiding clients through the application process for innocent spouse relief. They provide expert advice, ensure proper documentation, and help clients avoid common pitfalls. Ethical considerations are paramount, as specialists must represent their clients fairly and honestly, ensuring that all relevant information is accurately presented to the IRS.

CHAPTER 10

Payroll Issues

Payroll taxes are a significant concern for both employers and employees, and they play a crucial role in funding various government programs. In fact, IRS data reveals that eighty-five percent of taxes collected every year are from estimated income taxes, withholding taxes, and employer payroll taxes. For the purposes of this book, the payroll taxes referred to within are known as "trust fund" taxes. They consist of the Social Security, Medicare, federal income tax, and state income tax withholdings of each paycheck. The IRS likens the nonpayment of trust fund taxes to stealing from the government.

Payroll taxes are taxes imposed on employers and employees, typically calculated as a percentage of the wages that employers pay their staff. These taxes fund Social Security, Medicare, federal unemployment insurance, and other social programs. Employers are responsible for withholding these taxes from employees' wages and remitting them to the appropriate government agencies. Additionally, employers must match certain employee contributions, such as Social Security and Medicare taxes, in addition to federal and state unemployment taxes.

Payroll tax problems commonly occur in businesses with subpar accounting systems and internal controls. They manifest themselves into problems like poor internal and external payroll reporting, penalties due, failure to file and/ or pay taxes, trust fund recovery penalty assessments, worker misclassification audits, and full-blown payroll tax audits.

Payroll tax issues are symptomatic of a business owner who may not necessarily know how to run a business. They may be very accomplished at providing the goods or services in their field of expertise, but they fail in many of the basic functional areas of running a business, like managing cash flow. Business owners fail to understand, by and large, that the IRS is not like any other creditor who can "wait until the check clears" so they can get paid.

One such employer, an architect who was a client of mine, ran up a payroll tax bill of close to $300,000 under his corporation. This taxpayer was at risk of losing his business to the IRS due to poor internal controls and management. We had taken steps to make sure the IRS did not assess the trust fund recovery penalty, which may be assessed personally against the owner of the business. In this particular instance, it was fortunate that the IRS was not actively attempting to collect from the architect, buying us time to help him rearrange his business finances. We began by discussing how to better manage cash flow, and it reminded me of how these kinds of tax issues arise. It is the story of many business owners who run into these kinds of issues.

Cash flow management is so critical in any business, but even more so when payroll is involved and one of your creditors is the US Treasury. Perhaps he will now pay closer attention when the IRS makes him personally responsible for the company's payroll taxes. All it takes is one statutory notice delivered by certified mail or an on-site visit by a revenue officer from the local IRS office. It may not happen tomorrow, but the only thing accomplished by burying your head in the sand is that you leave everything else exposed!

The trust fund recovery penalty is imposed on individuals responsible for collecting, accounting for, and paying all employee withholdings to the IRS. This liability may be assessed against any individual the IRS deems as a responsible person. This includes all business owners, corporate officers, accounting personnel, and other potential responsible parties. Penalties for noncompliance can be substantial, including fines, interest, and potential criminal charges for intentional violations. The financial burden can be overwhelming, leading to business closures or bankruptcies in severe cases.

Understanding the common problems and implementing effective compliance strategies are essential for avoiding these issues. When problems arise, seeking professional help from a tax resolution specialist can make a significant difference in resolving the issues efficiently and minimizing the impact on the business.

CHAPTER 11
The Taxpayer Bill of Rights and the National Taxpayer Advocate

The Taxpayer Bill of Rights (TBOR) is a crucial framework established to protect taxpayers and ensure fair treatment by the IRS. Enacted to enhance transparency, accountability, and respect within the tax system, the TBOR outlines ten fundamental rights every taxpayer should be aware of and utilize when interacting with the IRS.

The TBOR's roots trace back to the Taxpayer Bill of Rights, originally enacted in 1988, followed by subsequent iterations in 1996 and 1998, which expanded and reinforced taxpayer protections. The most recent enhancement came in 2014 when the IRS adopted the current version of the TBOR, codifying these rights into a clear, concise format easily accessible to taxpayers. The TBOR is grounded in various sections of the Internal Revenue Code (IRC) and supported by IRS procedures and regulations designed to uphold these rights.

The Ten Fundamental Rights

1. **The Right to Be Informed:** Taxpayers have the right to a clear explanations of tax laws, IRS procedures, and their obligations. The IRS must provide accurate, accessible information to help taxpayers understand their responsibilities and the tax processes.

2. **The Right to Quality Service:** Taxpayers are entitled to prompt, courteous, and professional assistance from the IRS. This includes the right to receive clear communication and fair treatment in all interactions.

3. **The Right to Pay No More Than the Correct Amount of Tax:** Taxpayers should be liable for only the correct amount of tax due under the law. This right ensures that taxpayers are not overcharged and can dispute and rectify any errors in tax assessments.

4. **The Right to Challenge the IRS's Position and Be Heard:** Taxpayers can raise objections to IRS decisions and provide additional documentation or arguments. The IRS is obligated to consider these challenges promptly and fairly.

5. **The Right to Appeal an IRS Decision in an Independent Forum**: Taxpayers have the right to a fair and impartial administrative appeal of most IRS decisions, including many penalties, and the right to take their case to the US Tax Court if necessary.

6. **The Right to Finality**: Taxpayers are entitled to know the maximum time they have to challenge an IRS decision and the maximum time the IRS has to audit a particular tax year or collect a tax debt. This provides certainty and closure in tax matters.

7. **The Right to Privacy**: The IRS must respect taxpayer privacy and conduct investigations with minimal intrusion. These rights limit the IRS's ability to conduct unnecessary audits or investigations.

8. **The Right to Confidentiality**: Taxpayer information must be kept confidential. Unauthorized disclosure of tax information by the IRS is subject to legal consequences, ensuring the protection of personal data.

9. **The Right to Retain Representation**: Taxpayers can seek assistance from a qualified representative of their choice when dealing with the IRS. This right ensures that taxpayers can navigate complex tax issues with professional help.

10. **The Right to a Fair and Just Tax System:**
    Taxpayers have the right to expect fairness in tax
    administration. This includes the right to seek assis-
    tance from the Taxpayer Advocate Service (TAS) if
    they face financial difficulties or feel the system is
    not working as intended.

Each of these taxpayer rights plays a vital role in
protecting taxpayers and ensuring fair treatment. For
example, the *Right to Be Informed* empowers taxpayers to
understand and meet their tax obligations without fear of
arbitrary penalties. The *Right to Challenge the IRS's Position
and Be Heard* is crucial for resolving disputes, allowing
taxpayers to present their case and seek justice.

A small business owner who faces an unexpected
tax audit could utilize the *Right to Retain Representation*
to secure a tax resolution specialist's help, ensuring a fair
review and minimizing financial impact. Similarly, an individual wrongly assessed for additional taxes could leverage
the *Right to Appeal an IRS Decision in an Independent Forum*
to seek redress through the US Tax Court.

The IRS is committed to upholding the TBOR through
internal procedures and enforcement mechanisms. The TAS
plays a crucial role in this process, providing independent
assistance to taxpayers facing unresolved issues that cannot
be addressed through regular IRS channels.

The TAS was established to provide an independent voice within the IRS, with a twofold mission: to assist taxpayers in resolving their tax problems with the IRS and to identify and recommend solutions to systemic issues in the tax system. It operates under the leadership of the National Taxpayer Advocate (NTA), a position created by the Taxpayer Bill of Rights 2 in 1996. The NTA is responsible for overseeing the TAS and ensuring that it fulfills its mandate to advocate for taxpayer rights and address issues that impact taxpayers' ability to comply with tax obligations.

The TBOR is a cornerstone of fair tax administration in the United States. By outlining and enforcing these ten fundamental rights, the TBOR ensures that taxpayers are treated with respect, transparency, and fairness. As a tax resolution specialist, understanding and advocating for these rights is essential in protecting clients and ensuring justice in tax matters. Encouraging taxpayers to be proactive in understanding and exercising their rights can lead to more equitable outcomes and a more just tax system for all.

Understanding the role and functions of the TAS is also essential in providing comprehensive support to clients. By leveraging the resources and advocacy of the TAS, tax professionals can ensure that their clients receive fair treatment and their rights are protected throughout their interactions with the IRS.

CHAPTER 12
Next Steps

At the end of the day, being in tax trouble and having the IRS knocking on your door is a scary thing. It's a position no one wants to be in, but for the people I work with, it's often a position they couldn't do much to prevent themselves from getting into. Remember: Bad things can happen to good people. Sometimes we make tough decisions for good reasons because we're faced with hard times that require making those decisions. And sometimes, those decisions come back later to wreak havoc on us. That's just the way life goes, and paying our taxes is no exception to life's ups and downs in this way.

But just because something feels scary or inevitable doesn't mean it has to be the end of the world. You don't have to let your fear or lack of knowledge or misunderstanding about the situation paralyze you completely. In fact, you *can't* let it paralyze you completely, because inaction in the face of tax debt will only make matters worse. Knowledgeable action is your best friend in these circumstances.

That being the case, the best way forward is to gain the knowledge and partnerships you need in order to be as proactive for yourself as you can. That means reading books like this one to understand at least the basic concepts of what you're up against and what your options are. It also means doing the necessary research to find reputable tax resolution professionals, CPAs, or tax attorneys to put in your corner and help you wade through everything, whether it's before or after you find yourself in a bind. And the "research" portion of things is imperative because navigating these waters is a tough gig. This is a niche practice; not every CPA or lawyer can do it. To be even more truthful about it, not every CPA or lawyer is *willing* to do it. That's why a good tax resolution professional can often be such a rare breed to find.

But that's precisely why I take it upon myself to do this job. I believe in the Taxpayer Bill of Rights, and I do the work I do every day because I firmly believe in the societal duty that people have to pay their taxes as well as the right to be treated fairly by the associated government entities that legally owe you the opportunity to do the best you can with the hand you've been dealt. You have the right to pivot within the confines of the law when doing so becomes excessively challenging. Following the rule of law is the hallmark of an advanced society, and I believe in upholding every part of that society to follow those rules of law, for taxpaying citizens and government figureheads alike. And if you can understand and uphold the importance of that notion as well, you'll put yourself in a position of power that can either keep you out of tax trouble or help to get you out of tax trouble you might already be in.

That's another large part of why I do the work I do, and why nearly all my professional background leading up to this point has been in the world of finance in some form or fashion. I believe that we all have the tools we need to make smart decisions about our finances and keep ourselves out of tax trouble. If we each take the time to understand what our tax duties are and how they're meant to be paid to the government, there's no need for us to default on those payments and cause trouble for ourselves. We all have the means to make better financial decisions—whether it's figuring out how to earn more, save more, spend less, or allocate better—that can in turn help to keep us out of debt and ultimately, out of legal trouble.

So if you decide to start a business, then the onus is on you to understand what that means from a tax responsibility perspective and comply with it. If you decide you want to file your own taxes every tax season instead of hiring a professional to do it for you, that's your absolute right, but it then becomes your responsibility to make sure you're doing it correctly. We all have choices to make in life, and we have a responsibility to ourselves to make them as informed as possible.

If you take the time to understand the results and ramifications of the decisions you make and construct a plan for what those decisions may ultimately mean, you will give yourself so much more power in this life. And when bad things happen and tough decisions need to be made, then the next set of decisions to start considering is who you should turn to for help.

My hope is that this book has given you some of the knowledge and tools you need to fight the good fight and open your eyes to what your options might be if you don't want to fight your battles alone. I don't want the IRS trampling your rights. I don't want *anyone* trampling your rights—not even you. But if you don't give yourself the basics of knowledge you need to at least know what your rights and options are, then you might as well be stomping them right into the mud.

There are always options to combat the IRS when they behave as though they are unable to budge. The reality is more likely that they are unwilling to budge, not unable to—that, or their outdated processes, systems, and lines of thinking have caused them to make a mistake or have led them down the wrong path about you and your circumstances. I have seen that to be the case with many of my clients over the years.

So if you ever feel like something has gone amiss, or you aren't being treated fairly, then I encourage you to stand up and elevate the situation. Don't let them take that right away from you with dizzying hierarchies and confusing lingo. Don't let them hold all the power, no matter how hard they try to keep their hands—and theirs alone—on it. You have the ability to exhaust all your administrative and legal rights before bowing before them in full. And you have the right to work with someone like me to help make sure you're exhausting every avenue you can in order to find a resolution that works in your favor as much as possible.

Above all, I urge you to learn from everything you have experienced to this point. If you've been through tax trouble and come out the other side, or if you're currently in tax trouble and are wondering how you're going to get out of it, my biggest and brightest hope is that you will take valuable lessons away from your experience and use them to change your habits and other lines of thinking so that you can ultimately change your life for the better. Mistakes on the road of life are great kindling for doing things better the next time around. So let that fire-builder be you. Let your mistakes or misjudgments help you in this life, not hold you back even more than they already have.

If and when you've reached a point where the learning proves to be too difficult, where the processes and codes and laws and options all start to jumble into too large a knot to untie, then know that you always have experts to turn to. People like me are ready and waiting to help you loosen the knot and begin to straighten the string. You don't have to navigate through it alone, and it's possible that this book has shown you that you really shouldn't. But I also hope this book has proven to you just how much power you hold in your endeavors to resolve your tax debt. No one can take that away from you. Together, let's remind the powers that be of just how true that is.

If you or someone you know has unresolved tax issues with the IRS, The Tax Relief Pro may be able to help. Find out more about what we do or contact us directly through www.914tax.com or by calling (914) 712-6969.

ACKNOWLEDGMENTS

This book would not have been possible without the following acknowledgments:

I am eternally grateful to the Creator, who endows man with wisdom, insight, and discernment.

To the American Society of Tax Problem Solvers in Williamsville, NY. Their excellence in education and dedication to instruction make the practice of tax resolution all the more enjoyable and rewarding.

To all the taxpayers I have had the privilege to represent. Tax problems are a symptom of a larger behavioral problem regarding finances. They are a financial accident rarely seen coming. My role as a tax problem resolver is not only to help resolve the immediate problem at hand, but also to impart some lessons in tax financial management so that the problem doesn't reoccur.

To my beta readers for taking the time and making the effort not just to read my draft book, but for your detailed comments and feedback. This book is better because of you. You are my foxhole buddies.

To my sister, who inspired the title of the book.

Lastly, many thanks to Michael DeLon and his team at Paperback Expert, without whom this book would not be possible.

TAX TERMS DICTIONARY

Appeal: The legal process provided to seek additional judgment when a taxpayer has reasonable grounds to file a request to contest the IRS's decision about how or how much they will collect from a taxpayer in order to satisfy their debt.

Bankruptcy: The legal process through which an individual or business who cannot repay their debts may seek relief from some or all of their debts.

Certified Public Accountant (CPA): A licensed accountant who is qualified to provide accounting services to the public.

Chapter 7 Bankruptcy: A type of liquidation bankruptcy wherein a trustee is appointed by the court to handle selling property and assets to attempt to partially pay off debts or repay creditors.

Chapter 13 Bankruptcy: A type of bankruptcy that allows for a plan to repay all or part of an individual's debts over a period of three to five years. It does not require liquidating assets.

Collection Appeals Program (CAP): A reactive measure a taxpayer can take when they receive notice of a penalty and a specific collection action to be taken from the IRS. It allows the taxpayer to seek to appeal the enforcement procedures and provides them with an opportunity to suggest an alternative to the proposed debt collection. The taxpayer generally has thirty days to request CAP.

Collection Due Process (CDP) Hearing: A reactive response to the "final" notice of collection provided by the IRS. It is more often used when a notice of federal lien or intent to levy is given. The taxpayer generally has ninety days to request a CDP hearing.

Collection Due Process (CDP) Equivalent Hearing: If a taxpayer misses the 90-day deadline to file a CDP hearing, they may still have the opportunity to file it via a CDP Equivalent hearing, but in doing so, the taxpayer will forfeit their opportunity to proceed to Tax Court.

Collection Statute Expiration Date (CSED): A limit on the length of time the government has to collect any tax debt that's owed for any particular tax year, most commonly ten years.

Currently Not Collectible (CNC): If a taxpayer owes tax debt in an amount that proves too difficult to manage in any capacity according to their current life situation, they may qualify as CNC, which puts a pause on collection but does not remove it.

Equitable Tolling: The Tax Court's discretionary extension of a deadline surrounding certain tax payments, collection processes, or other time-sensitive elements. It is most often granted when the taxpayer was somehow prevented from complying with the set deadline despite their best efforts to do so.

Federal Tax Lien: Also sometimes referred to as simply a lien, this is the government's legal claim against a taxpayer's property or finances, which protects their interest in it if they intend to claim it when the taxpayer owes a tax debt.

Garnishment: A seizure of funds usually associated with the earned wages or income of the taxpayer. A continuous portion of their regular income is collected as part of a debt owed to the government until the debt is satisfied.

Installment Agreement (IA): Also sometimes referred to as a payment plan, an installment agreement allows a taxpayer to pay their entire balance owed to the IRS in smaller installments over time rather than in the full sum in one payment.

Internal Revenue Service (IRS): A branch of the US Department of the Treasury established as a means to assess and collect the taxes legally owed by American citizens.

Judgment: A court decision that provides a resolution to a problem presented in a hearing. When a taxpayer is either unable or unwilling to pay their debt or come up with agreeable alternate arrangements for both parties, the IRS may remove the taxpayer's case from the Tax Court so it can proceed to a federal court, whereby the taxpayer will be required to resolve their tax debt even beyond any expiration of any CSEDs in place so that the debt can be completely resolved.

Levy: The legal seizure of a taxpayer's property in order to satisfy a debt. Personal bank or financial accounts can be used to pay the amount owed or physical property valued at the amount of the debt can be seized in lieu of monetary funds.

Nonfiler: A taxpayer who has not filed one or more income tax returns with the IRS as legally required.

Nonpriority Debt: A type of unsecured debt that is only paid off after all priority debts have been paid first. Examples include credit card debt, medical debt, back rent, utility bills, and union dues.

Offer in Compromise (OIC): An agreement between the indebted taxpayer and the IRS to settle the taxpayer's debt for less than they originally owed, and usually in one lump-sum payment rather than in installments over time.

Partial Payment Installment Agreement (PPIA): A type of payment plan with the IRS that allows a taxpayer to pay back only part of the taxes owed via monthly payments until their tax liability expires according to the CSED.

Payment Arrangements: An enforced collection method that may allow the taxpayer to pay their debt to the IRS in installments rather than in one lump sum and may sometimes require payment in full or in part over an extended period of time.

Payroll Taxes: A trust fund tax that a business owner acts as the custodian of by withholding the taxes from their employees' regular paychecks and then sending them to the US government in order to contribute to public programs such as Social Security and Medicare.

Priority Debt: A type of unsecured debt that must be paid off before nonpriority debts are paid off. Examples include wages owed to employees, alimony or child support, and penalties owed to the government.

Secured Debt: A type of debt that has some kind of collateral property securing the debt, making it so that if the borrower defaults on the debt, the creditor can take the property from them. Examples include mortgages and car loans.

Seizure: The act of forcibly collecting property or finances from the indebted taxpayer by the IRS.

Statutory Notice of Deficiency (SNOD): Sometimes also called a statutory notice or a ninety-day letter, this is a legal notice issued by the government informing the taxpayer of their proposed tax deficiency and providing them the right to petition the US Tax Court.

Substitute for Return (SFR): An internal document the IRS will compile in place of a nonfiler's missing tax return. It is not considered a replacement for a taxpayer-filed return and is instead used as a means for the IRS to determine how much the nonfiler owes in taxes when there is no return to provide guidance.

Tagging: A type of enforced collection whereby a piece of property isn't yet taken out of the taxpayer's possession and is instead "tagged" as property of the US government as a means of marking it as inaccessible or unusable, or otherwise physically making it inaccessible to the taxpayer until a debt can be collected.

Tax Court: A US federal court system established by Congress to provide a judicial forum where individuals and other entities can contest a tax deficiency that has been determined by the IRS.

Tax Resolution Specialist: A finance and/or law professional qualified and trained specifically in helping individuals and businesses manage their tax problems.

Taxable Income: Any type of money paid for work or a service such as wages, interest, dividends, or any other type of compensation on which the US tax system imposes a tax.

Unsecured Debt: A type of debt that does not have some kind of property or asset serving as collateral for the debt. Examples include credit card debt, student loans, medical debt, back payments on rent, and utility bills.

ABOUT RON FRIEDMAN, CPA, CTRS

A graduate of City University of New York-Queen College campus and St. John's University-Jamaica campus, Ron Friedman, "the Tax Relief Pro," has been a licensed New York State Certified Public Accountant since 2000 and holds the Certified Tax Resolution Specialist designation from the American Society of Tax Problem Solvers, a designation few CPAs have.

Ron has spoken in front of industry trade groups in matters of tax planning and tax resolution, and he has hosted his own public radio show, "Tax Tips with Ron Friedman." He is also a member in good standing of the American Institute of CPAs, the New York State Society of CPAs, and the American Society of Tax Problem Solvers, a nation-wide, not-for-profit professional association dedicated to the training and education of tax problem solvers. He is also a past recipient of the Top Practitioner Award presented by the American Society of Problem Solvers.

To learn more about Ron and his business, The Tax Relief Pro, or to see how he might be able to help you resolve your tax problems, visit **www.914tax.com.**